INSTRUCTIONS

FOR

BRITISH
SERVICEMEN

IN

FRANCE
1944

ISBN 1-85124-335-6
@Bodleian Library, University of Oxford, 2005
All rights reserved
Designed by Dot Little
Typeset by Melanie Gradtke
Printed by Cromwell Press, Trowbridge, Wiltshire

British Library Cataloguing in Publication Data
A CIP record of this publication is available from the British Library

CONTENTS

EDITOR'S NOTE

This edition reproduces the spelling of the original, except in the case of ize/ise spellings, which have been regularized. The section entitled 'Words and Phrases' is printed in abridged form.

PREFACE

A draft of this pamphlet, stamped 'Confidential' and called 'Soldiers' Guide to France', survives, alongside a copy of the work as published, in the papers of the journalist Herbert David Ziman, which were given to the Bodleian in 1995 by his daughters, Elizabeth Ziman and Naomi Roberts. Ziman was on the staff of the *Daily Telegraph* for 35 years, as leader-writer, war correspondent and finally, from 1956 to 1968, as literary editor and special correspondent throughout the world. Having served with the Artists' Rifles for four years before the outbreak of war, he was called up in September 1939 and joined the Middlesex Regiment. We learn from a *curriculum vitae* which he drew up in 1947 that, during secondment from the Intelligence Corps to the French Section of the Political Warfare Executive in 1943, he wrote 'the little pamphlet on France issued to troops for the invasion'.

It is a remarkable little pamphlet, demonstrating both a wide-ranging knowledge of France and a deep sympathy for the French people. The opening quotation from Churchill in August 1943 on the certainty of France rising again 'free, united and independent', sets the scene for what follows: the upbeat summaries of French history and geography, the lively survey of national and regional characteristics, the section of useful French phrases (of which only a flavour is given here), the conversion of metric measures, the explanation of road signs and the final grave warning about the risk of sabotage and the importance of the strictest security. Although essentially a set of instructions to British servicemen in the Second World War on how to behave to the civilian population in a foreign country, its blend of commonsense and humanity makes it a document of enduring interest.

It is fascinating to compare this pamphlet with the *Instructions for American Servicemen in Britain 1942* (Bodleian Library, 2004). They have much in common. Both consider it necessary to rehearse the basics of considerate behaviour abroad, including avoidance of political argument, criticism of local customs and over-enthusiastic acceptance of hospitality in countries where food is scarce and rationed. British servicemen are told to 'be natural, but don't make yourself too much at home till you are sure your French friends like it', and the Americans are advised to 'be friendly, but don't intrude anywhere it seems you are not wanted'. The British are given a three-page summary of the history of France and told that throughout the sixteenth, seventeenth and eighteenth centuries the French were not only the dominant power in Europe, but also the chief cultural and civilising influence; while the Americans are reminded that Britain is the cradle of democracy and of many American liberties. It takes two pages to instruct the British soldiers on how France was governed before the occupation. Americans are told simply that the old monarchical power has shifted to the Parliament, Prime Minister and Cabinet, but are warned 'NEVER' to criticise the King or Queen.

In an article in the Daily Express of 9 June 1944, just three days after D-Day, J. M. Cameron wrote that, far from being a 'school-masterish' set of instructions or 'a Cook's appendix to the King's Regulations', the Soldiers' Guide was 'the gentlest and most human article the soldier carries to the wars'. The suffering of the French people during four years of enemy occupation is a recurring theme in the pamphlet, as is the need to move on from the collapse of France in June 1940 and to recognize the achievements and sacrifices of the French Resistance. The frequent references to the events of 1940 reflect their importance in shaping contemporary opinion in Britain about France and the French. Similarly the sections on the French, their culture and their way of life are as revealing of British attitudes as they are of those of their allies across the Channel. As Cameron shrewdly pointed out, the pamphlet was 'probably the only guide to foreign parts which holds up the mirror not to the place, but to the visitor'. For example, an instruction not to drink too much alcohol is accompanied by the information that there was always less drunkenness in pre-war France than in England, and that the inability of some British troops to 'take their wine' was 'the one point made against our men in France in 1939–40 and in North Africa'. Again, soldiers in the British Expeditionary Force in 1944 are warned to guard against the thoughtlessness of some British peace-time visitors whose behaviour implied that nowhere abroad came up to their standards or expectations.

As a document reflecting the enduring problems of war, oc-cupation and invasion, the pamphlet continues to be of interest long after it has served its original purpose. In particular for the millions of British who, since the end of the Second World War have holidayed or settled in France, it offers a fascinating glimpse of France herself and of British attitudes to France at a crucial time in the history of both countries, an instructive guide against which to measure contemporary cross-Channel relations.

Mary Clapinson
Senior Research Fellow
St. Hugh's College, Oxford
2005

INSTRUCTIONS
FOR
BRITISH SERVICEMEN
IN
FRANCE

Prepared by
The Political Warfare Executive

Issued by
The Foreign Office, London

1944

This book has nothing to do with military operations. It deals only with civilian life in France and with the way you should behave to the French civilian population.

"*You may be sure that France will rise again free, united, and independent, to stand on guard with others over the generous tolerances and brightening opportunities of the human society we mean to rescue and rebuild.*"

MR. CHURCHILL
(Aug. 31st, 1943)

—FRANCE—

A NEW B.E.F., which includes you, is going to France. You are to assist personally in pushing the Germans out of France and back where they belong. In the process, you will meet the French, maybe not for the first time. You will also, almost certainly for the first time, be seeing a country which has been subjected to German occupation for several years. This is a point worth fixing in your mind. You will learn what it means.

The pages which follow are devoted to the French and not the Germans, who have incidentally behaved far worse in other countries than in France. Indeed, the individual German soldier has behaved, on the whole, remarkably correctly in France. He was ordered to do so. It was part of a plan for winning France over to the Nazi "New Order" for Europe. But the French have *not* been won over. They have had a long and painful lesson in what the "New Order" means. Their one desire has been, and is, to get the Germans and the "New Order" out. You will be left in no doubt that they welcome your help in achieving this. But the results of the German occupation are likely to be seen even in the way you are welcomed: the French will give you as good a welcome as they can, but the last few years have made this difficult, as you will realize as soon as you read on.

Remember that continental France has been directly occupied. In consequence it has been stripped of everything by the Germans. Almost all French civilians (including French children) are undernourished, and many have died from exhaustion and hunger, because the Germans have eaten the food. The Germans have also drunk the wine or distilled it into engine-fuel. So there are only empty barrels to roll.

You have known something of rationing at home, and seen temporary shortages of various things to which you were accustomed. But you have never known, as the French, thanks to the Germans, have known, a lasting dearth of the commonest articles. Food, drink, clothes, tobacco—everything has been rationed, but to have a coupon has not meant to get even the meagre ration. Women have queued up daily for vegetables from four in the morning till the market closed at 8.30—and gone away without any because the Germans had robbed the lorries on the way. Bread has often been unobtainable and often nearly uneatable. There have been minute rations of a soap which will not wash. Simple necessities like bandages or baby-foods or condensed milk have been unobtainable. Cigarettes have been rationed to three a day—when they were available at all. The towns have suffered worst, but the country districts have not escaped lightly. Short or non-existent rations have, of course, been supplemented by black market activities. Some of the activities have been designed to keep food out of German hands, and have had general approval of patriotic Frenchmen. Others have amounted to black market selling and buying as we know it for the benefit of profiteers and those with enough money to buy at the expense of their poorer countrymen.

EFFECTS ON THE FRENCH.—So the French, after the German occupation, are, generally speaking, in no position to entertain you lavishly, though families may get up from the cellar in our special honour a long-hidden bottle. If so, remember that it may be the last they have. A good many people are likely in any case to lack the energy or the mood to do much "celebrating," however great their joy and relief at being freed. When anyone has been living for a long time suffering from privation or in a concentration camp, and is suddenly let out, it takes him time to recuperate. And France had developed under the German occupation much of the physical depression of a huge sick-room, and much of the mental stress of a huge concentration camp.

Lack of food, lack of medicines, lack of soap and towels have spread disease in France to an extent previously unheard of. A recent French estimate suggests that as many as one in twelve of the population may be suffering from tuberculosis. Cases of syphilis were most frequent in the neighbourhood of German military centres and may be as many as one in eight of the population. As for the spirit of the concentration camp, two-thirds of France has been ruled directly by the German army and the Gestapo since June, 1940. The rest of France was indirectly controlled by a Quisling Government at Vichy until November, 1942, when the Germans occupied this portion too. The Vichy Government was then allowed to carry on as a local administration. The Germans and their Vichy henchmen introduced all the blessings of the "New Order." Getting on for a million Frenchmen (apart from 1¼ million prisoners of war) have been deported to Germany. Another 150,000 have been in actual prisons or concentration camps in France. **Each year at least 5,000 Frenchmen have been shot for active resistance—one very two hours.** This includes anything from derailing a German troop-train to helping British soldiers or airmen escape.

HELPING OUR MEN ESCAPE.—For security reasons we have not heard much about the help which French civilians, at the risk of their lives, have given British soldiers and airmen since the 1940 Armistice. But it is a thing we should remember with the utmost gratitude. The controlled Press and Radio in France have been dinning anti-British propaganda into French minds ever since 1940, accusing us of betraying France and then trying to seize her Empire. These stories have been answered only by the B.B.C. French broadcasts (to which the French are forbidden to listen), by leaflets dropped by the R.A.F. and the Americans (which it is forbidden to pass on), and by the "underground" newspapers run (again at the risk of their lives) by French patriots. **Yet the ordinary Frenchman and Frenchwoman have never ceased to regard us as their allies.** They have sheltered and fed (often at great personal sacrifice) hundreds of British soldiers and airmen, and passed them right through the country and across neutral frontiers, knowing all the time that their own lives were forfeit if they were discovered.

One motive which encouraged them to take these risks, apart from French patriotism, was certainly the popularity which British troops earned in France between 1914 and 1918, and again in 1939–40. Those of us who were there at the time remember many acts of kindness received from the French, and many small courtesies which we were able to offer in return. We must always remember that we have twice fought together in this century on the soil of France: British cemeteries, if you see them, are a permanent reminder. On this, the third time, we shall get less generous hospitality, just because the Germans have stripped France. But the present British Army is unlikely to behave less well to the French than earlier British expeditionary forces. Indeed, we have reason to show even greater consideration. For the individual German soldier in France has been outwardly very "correct," on the strictest orders. He almost overbalanced, at least at the beginning, in his contortions to appear friendly—but without thereby winning the regard of the French. **We owe it to our self-respect as British soldiers to show ourselves really well-behaved in every way. But we, unlike the Germans, can be naturally friendly, seeing that the French are naturally our friends.**

One word of warning. If you are among the first to land in France, your welcome will be of the warmest. But if you are a few weeks after the first troops, and if Allied assistance to the French population—food, clothing, etc.—has appeared to them slow in coming, there may be a slight reaction. Remember then, if tackled on the subject, to say that we are doing our best, and all eventually will be well. For that will be the plain truth: after all, the war has hit us, too.

WHAT WOULD YOU FEEL?—You will find in this book a few special "tips" on how to behave to the French. But your principal guide is, of course, your own common sense, coupled with your imagination of what *you* would be feeling about friendly foreign troops in your own town or village. Your own people at home must have told you that both British and allied units in their neighbourhood vary considerably in their conduct. Most of them make themselves welcome guests. But some make themselves just a nuisance which has to be endured. One way troops in England can become unpopular, through mere thoughtlessness, is by purchasing in the local shops things which are scarce, so that civilians go short. **In the first months you will almost certainly find in France such shortage that it will be up to you not to try to buy anything, much less scrounge.** An unimportant comfort for a British soldier will be an absolute necessity to some Frenchman. And buying food at a farm may quite likely mean preventing some child in the nearest town from getting a meal.

Above all, have nothing to do with any black market. Whatever the temptation, buying on this simply means that the poor who need food will not get it, and the return to normal distribution will be complicated and delayed.

There is another kind of thoughtlessness, which some

of us may have to watch, though it is commoner among British peace-time visitors abroad than among British soldiers. It consists of airing the opinion that such and such a foreign country or town or village is very lucky to have chaps like us passing through. Of course, no one is such a fool as to put the thing bluntly in words like that. But it is amazing how many people (not all, of course, British, or all outside their own country) can imply by their whole manner that the world in general, and the place where they have just arrived in particular, hardly come up to their standards. Well, that kind of attitude, however innocently silly, will be out of place in France. The French accept foreign visitors, which includes us, pretty readily, and they had before the war 3,000,000 foreign residents living among 39,000,000 French people. But they were not particularly impressed by foreigners, or very interested in them. What interested Frenchmen was, and is, France: they think that France is a very great country, with a great record of civilization—and they have every reason to think so.

—THE COUNTRY—

FRANCE is a country of over 212,000 square miles, i.e. nearly 2½ times the size of our island. Until Hitler began to sprawl over his neighbours, France was the largest country in Europe outside Russia. It has rivers much longer than our own Thames, and more and higher mountains than can be found in Britain. And whereas we have the sea as our frontier all round, France has nearly 2,000 miles of coast and almost the same length of land-frontiers. These land-frontiers make France far more a continental than a maritime Power. Neither the French navy, nearly as large as our own and thoroughly efficient in 1939, nor the fine French mercantile marine and fishing fleets, nor the possession of an Empire overseas second only to the British Empire, has made French-men in the mass think of the sea as a really important element in the nation's existence. For it is only over the land-frontiers that any direct threat to the nation has come in recent centuries.

When French schoolboys sketch a freehand outline of their country, they start by drawing a six-sided hex-agonal figure.

The shape of France then fits fairly easily within this framework. An imaginary tour round this figure, anti-clockwise, starting at the top (northern-most) corner, would go first along the edge which faces us across the Channel, past Dunkirk, Calais, Boulogne, Dieppe, Havre, Cherbourg (jutting out on a peninsula like a thumb), St. Malo, and in the north-west corner (Brittany) Brest. Then the western "side" makes a great curve forming the Bay of Biscay—and containing the Atlantic ports of Lorient, St. Nazaire, La Rochelle and Bordeaux. Next comes the mountain frontier with Spain—the Pyrenees. You have now covered three of your six sides.

Follow the next stage—France's Mediterranean coast, with the inward curve of the Gulf of Lions and the mouth of the Rhône, then an outward curve taking in Marseilles and Toulon and ending on the east with the Riviera, where the Alps come down to the sea. Next, northwards along a very jagged "side"—the Alpine boundary first with Italy, then with Switzerland. The frontier begins to turn into another mountain range, the Jura, and then the Rhine boundary with Germany, protected on the French side by the Vosges mountains. So far you have followed the natural frontiers, but along the final stage you follow the unprotected north-eastern edge of France, touching in turn Germany, Luxembourg and Belgium.

NORTH-EAST FRONTIER.—It is this frontier which the Germans crossed in 1870, in 1914 and again in 1940—there are people in France who have suffered three German invasions!; and it was because of this frontier, and, of course, because of German ambitions and German strength, that the French were forced to introduce conscription as long ago as at the time of the Revolution, generations before we did this. The southern frontier of France, with Spain, has been settled for nearly 300 years. The eastern frontier with Italy was fixed in 1860. The north-eastern frontier has changed many times through the centuries.

A few years before the war the French started to protect this vulnerable flank with the Maginot Line, which most of us thought was so strong that the Germans could not get into France this time. However strong, it was not long enough; for from where the Belgian frontier begins at Longwy, to the sea nearly 300 miles away, no Maignot Line had been built. It was believed that the Germans would not invade Belgium again, or that the Belgians would be strong enough to stop them. Both ideas were wrong. France was invaded once more.

BRITISH HISTORY begins with a succession of invasions from abroad. Since 1066 no one has ever invaded our island. In France, which is not an island, the invasions have continued to our own times, and the 1940 invasion was the third within living memory. That is one reason why the French, starting not unlike ourselves, have developed rather differently.

Roughly 2,000 years ago, just before the Romans came, France and Britain were peopled by closely related races—the Gauls and the Ancient Britons.

In both countries the Romans failed to penetrate to the outlying corners, but their domination of France was more complete and lasting. They left more imposing monuments, particularly in the south—temples, aqueducts, arenas. The Romans also left much of their customs, their laws and their language. These were adopted by the Franks, the next invaders of France, whereas we in Britain got a different system of laws and a different language brought in by the Angles and Saxons.

NORMANS AND ENGLISH.—Curiously enough the next great invasion also had quite different effects in the two countries. The Danes who raided and settled in England became absorbed. The Norsemen, Viking cousins of the Danes, raided France but finally settled in a compact body in Normandy. Though they adopted the French language and ways, they remained for a long time politically distinct. It was a Norman and not a French invasion of England which was led by William the Conqueror, and for two centuries the Kings of England, in their role as Dukes of Normandy, where highly independent and warlike vassals of the Kings of France.

On and off throughout the Middle Ages the Kings of France were in conflict with Germans, Austrians, Italians, Spaniards and Swiss—and with independent principalities inside France's borders. The long wars with England and the recurrent invasions from our side of the Channel have left the modern Frenchman with no grudge against us, except perhaps for the burning of Joan of Arc.

BEFORE THE REVOLUTION.—You may like to have some picture of what happened in France before the French revolution of 1789. Here is a rough idea:—

16th century: Wars with foreign powers (chiefly the Austrian Hapsburg Emperors). Then civil wars (Catholics against Protestants).

17th century: Climax of French monarchy and great age of French literature and art. Colonization abroad and wars in Europe.[1]

---

[1] Practically all the modern French Colonies have been acquired in the last 70 years.

16

18th century: More wars in Europe. Most of the French colonies lost in wars with Britain. The monarchy collapses, not through its tyranny but from its inefficiency.

During this period, France was not only the dominant power in Europe, but the chief cultural and civilizing influence.

The French Revolution was not, of course, a Communist revolution or even mainly a revolution of the poor against the rich. It was a revolution of the prosperous middle-classes who have led France ever since against an aristocracy which had already ceased to lead. Neighbouring continental kingdoms with aristocratic governments became alarmed and tried to restore the French monarchy. The Revolutionary French Republic retorted with a general campaign against foreign monarchs. Britain became involved in one more war with France. It went on (with two short pauses) from 1793 to 1815.

FRANCE SINCE 1815.— Since Waterloo France and Britain have never again been at war. They have fought together as allies three times—in the Crimean war and in the two world wars against Germany. After Napoleon's fall in 1815, the monarchy was restored in France. It was unsettled and short-lived, and finally after a brief experiment in constitutional monarchy beginning in 1830, it collapsed in 1848. There followed the even short-lived

Second Republic whose President, Louis-Bonaparte, had himself made Emperor under the title of Napoleon 3rd in 1852. During the Second Empire, France laid the foundations of her modern colonial Empire, which was later added to and consolidated under the Third Republic. The Second Empire came to and end with Napoleon's abdication in 1870 after the disastrous France-Prussian war (the first of those three German invasions which Frenchmen still living to-day can remember, and which explain the deep-rooted fear and hatred of Germany throughout France). Since that date, and until the setting up of the Vichy régime in 1940, France has lived under the Third Republic.

By comparison with the outwardly settled forms of British government during the same period, the history of France in the nineteenth century consisted of a series of political upheavals. But underneath all the changes of government the live forces of French democracy remained strong and active. Universal suffrage, introduced in 1848, came earlier in France than in Britain and survived all the anti-democratic measures of the Second Empire. Political and personal liberty, fought for in a series of bitter struggles, remain vital possessions for Frenchmen. Attempts to interfere with either meet unfailingly with a vigorous reaction. Of the original slogan of the French Revolution, "liberty" and "equality" have never ceased to preoccupy Frenchmen, often at the expense of national "fraternity".

FRENCHMEN have, of course, a strong *national* feeling—a pride in being, as a united France, so long a dominant force in Europe. But you may also notice among them a *regional* loyalty to the part of France from which they come. This "regionalism" is partly derived from the old separate feudal principalities and dukedoms, partly from racial differences. For the French nation includes other groups as distinct from each other as the Bretons and Normans—for instance the Basques of the South-West, who have a peculiar language of their own, the Catalans at the other end of the Pyrenees, and the people of Provence, inland from Marseilles. Even in those parts of France which have not a separate language of their own there is usually a regional dialect called a "patois" which the peasants prefer to speak rather than the French of the grammar-books.[1]

This regional feeling does not imply any weakening of the national spirit. Alsace and Lorraine (whose inhabitants largely speak a kind of German dialect) joined France less than three centuries ago, and were torn away by the Germans from 1870 to 1918. None the less the Alsatians and Lorrainers, to-day temporarily under German rule once more, are chafing to become French

[1] They understand "good" French none the less.

subjects again. It is even more remarkable that Savoy, which joined France as recently as 1860, is the main stronghold in which young Frenchmen in thousands have held out in the hills for months to avoid being deported to Germany as "factory-fodder". Evidently France creates French patriotism in its citizens very quickly. But it does not run them into one single type, and it would be difficult to point to a "typical" Frenchman. You yourself, if you first meet the French in the North of France, may easily jump to the conclusion that all Frenchmen are surprisingly silent and dour. If you are in the South of France, you are more likely to think of all Frenchmen as very lively and talkative. Either of these first impressions would be changed if you saw more of France.

ATTACHED TO THE LAND.—All the same, you can make certain generalizations about the French, and the first is their attachment to the land. Before the war over half of the population lived "on the land" or in small country towns. Almost all countrymen, and many townsmen as well, owned and cultivated a small piece of property, even if they also worked for an employer. This widespread ownership of land has given Frenchmen a distinct twist towards individualism. This is helped by the fact that though there are, of course, big industries in France, small firms and independent craftsmen are very common.

The bitterness of French social conflicts in the last years before 1939 and the frequency of strikes were largely due to political quarrels and the comparative newness of large-scale industry and organized trade unionism. Class distinctions are not very obvious in France. The old social castes were largely swept away by the French Revolution, and the Revolution's key-words, "Liberty, Equality and Fraternity", have at least reduced social snobbery to a minimum. Every Frenchman likes to feel himself as good as his neighbours. He would consider himself insulted if a stranger did not call him "Monsieur" ("Sir").

In general the French earned less money than we did in similar occupations—and worked longer hours for it. They spent less on their clothes and the decoration of their homes, less on travel and entertainment. But common sense and good cooking probably made the average French clerk's or workman's home more comfortable than that of many Englishmen of the same status. If it sometimes had fewer or smaller rooms, this did not matter much, since the Frenchman entertained his acquaintances in cafés or restaurants. You had to be a close friend before he asked you home. To-day, of course, the comfort and the good food, thanks to the German occupation, have vanished and he has been unable to replace his worn clothes. Do not judge by present appearances, or remark on "bad housing" when what you actually find is poor sanitation and lack of repairs.

By and large, Frenchmen, whatever their income or job, are inclined to what we would call a "middle-class" view of life. They are outwardly politer than most of us, and they enjoy and intellectual argument more than we do. You will often think that two Frenchmen are having a violent quarrel when they are simply arguing some abstract point. The excitement is all on the surface; fundamentally they are at least as tolerant as ourselves.

The French, however, are not tolerant of authority—as the Germans have found to their cost. Their first reaction to a uniform or a regulation is not to obey unquestioningly, but rather to ask whether it is necessary and make disrespectful comments if they decide it is not. This is all part of the Frenchman's deep belief in the individual. He is convinced of his right to think for himself and voice his criticisms aloud.

RELIGION AND ART.—The need for tolerance was taught the French by the religious wars and persecutions of earlier times. To-day the vast majority are Roman Catholics, with about a million Protestants. And though many French people call themselves "free-thinkers", you will probably find French parish churches better attended than most English churches. Roman Catholic clergy do not marry. The parish priest[1] in France is even less well-paid than an English parson. He feels it quite natural to live like the "people" rather than the "gentry"; he is usually a man of weight and influence locally, and he is called up for combatant service like any other Frenchman.

The cathedrals, churches and abbeys provide an impressive memorial both of French religious life and of French craftsmanship. Some are built in the very solid-looking "Norman" style, with round arches and thick pillars, others in the more graceful "Gothic" with pointed arches. The older public buildings, too, are often remarkable even in a comparatively small French town. Just because they have been less of an industrial nation than ourselves, the French have destroyed fewer fine buildings in "improvement" schemes. The ordinary Frenchman is, indeed, without losing his practical point of view, usually more conscious of art than the ordinary Englishman. You will find French painters, both Old Masters and modern artists, taken seriously by more of their fellow-countrymen than our own great artists are in Britain. But if you yourself are interested in art, you may be surprised to find how little Frenchmen know about British painters.

---

[1] It is somewhat confusing for us that the vicar is called the "curé" and the curate is called the "vicaire".

FAMILY LIFE.—In normal times the French have a family life rather less free-and-easy than the life of a British household. The father is very decidedly head of the family and exercises authority over his grown-up children, particularly daughters, in a way which has gone out of fashion in our country. Women in France, even in peacetime, work on the land and in the factories to an extent reached by women in Britain only in time of war. In 1918 the wartime work of the British women was made a reason for giving women the vote. Nothing similar has yet occurred in France, and the French-woman has shared in ruling modern France only, but very effectively, through her influence in every way on her menfolk.

Thanks to jokes about "Gay Paree", "French fares", and "Pictures from Paris", there is a fairly widespread belief among people in Britain that the French are a particularly gay, frivolous people with no morals and few convictions. This is especially untrue at the present time, when the French have been living a life of hardship and suffering. But the idea of the French living a in glorious orgy of "wine, women and song" never was true, even before the war. The French drink wine as we drink beer. It is the national drink and a very good drink, but there was far less drunkenness in peacetime in France than in peacetime England.

NOT LIKE MONTMARTRE.—It is also as well to drop any ideas about French women based on stories of Montmartre and nude cabaret shows. These were always designed as a tourist-attraction for foreigners; in Paris in peacetime one saw far more British and American (and Germans) than Frenchmen at the famous Folies Bergères. If you should happen to imagine that the first pretty French girl who smiles at you intends to dance the can-can or take you to bed, you will risk stirring up a lot of trouble for yourself—and for our relations with the French.

Like us, the French are on the whole a conventional people. But it happens that their conventions differ in some respects from ours. Some British peacetime visitors to France were shocked to find that the French had licensed brothels. Well, French visitors to Britain have been sometimes equally shocked by couples love-making publicly in our parks. The men may relieve nature rather openly in public and see little harm in frankness on various matters. But French people are rather startled when they hear a music-hall comedian in this country joking about "nancy-boys" or see some of us, "with drink taken", badly out of control. We are not the only nation to feel more virtuous than our neighbours, or to criticize their morals. The French do the same with regard to us. It is perhaps characteristic that what we call "taking French leave", the French call *"filer à l'anglaise"*.

—HOW FRANCE WAS GOVERNED—

BEFORE the war the French Republic had at its head a President, who, broadly speaking, "reigned" like our King, but with the important difference that he was *elected* and served as head of the State only for seven years. There was a Senate, rather like our House of Lords[1] but again elected, and an elected Chamber of Deputies, rather like our own House of Commons. Instead of our three main parties—Conservatives, Liberals and Socialists—the French had large number of parties. The French Socialist party was much smaller than ours—and the French Communist party more numerous than our Communists. The names of French political parties were very misleading to foreigners. For instance, what we call "Liberals" the French called "Radical Socialists". In any case, both the names and the parties they represented may well have been replaced by new ones by the time you get to France.

Largely because there were so many parties the pre-war French political system did not work very smoothly. Cabinets lasted sometimes only a few days and seldom for more than a year. Many French politicians (for instance Laval, who leads the Vichy Quisling Government) gained a bad name for corruption and double-dealing.

---

[1] There are herdiatry titles in France, relics of pre-Republican days, but it is a mere coincidence if a French Duke or Viscount is also a Senator.

While the Vichy system, which replaced the pre-1940 Republic, will certainly not survive, the old politicians are unlikely to come back to power. Nor is the old Republican constitution likely to be fully restored. **However, the questions of who will come into power and what sort of constitution France will have are entirely matters for Frenchmen to decide when France is freed.** Many Frenchmen have very strong feelings on this subject. Much will obviously depend upon the men who have led resistance to the Germans in France since 1940, risking their lives for years as dangerously as a soldier risks his life in battle.

LOCAL AUTHORITIES.—Without butting into French politics, you will want to know something about the local authorities. For however the country may be temporarily run in the areas occupied by Allied armies, we shall still need to respect the system which exists. This system depends on the French county, which is called a "Département". (There are 90 of them, including Corsica.) The chief official in the Département is called the Prefect and he is nominated by the French Government, just as in Britain the Lord Lieutenant is appointed by the King. The Prefect is, however, unlike the Lord Lieutenant, a paid full-time official with very wide powers. You are unlikely to come across him in person.

If you do, remember that he is a most important man, to be treated with respect.

Below the Département are smaller local groupings, called Arrondissements, Cantons and finally Communes. The Commune is the equivalent of the English town council, urban district council or rural district council, and at its head is always and elected "Maire" (Mayor). It is with the Maire that a unit is most likely to deal over local problems like billets, traffic accidents or entertainments. If you arrange a football match it will always be a good idea to invite "Monsieur le Maire". He will almost certainly be delighted to come.

FRENCH LAW.—Besides being France's greatest military genius, Napoleon was also her greatest law-giver. The code of laws which he established, the Code Napoleon, lasted in France, with amendments, through the nineteenth century and left a great mark on many of the legal systems of Europe. It outlived two monarchies, the Second Republic, the Second Empire and the Third Republic. Napoleon's system of laws is nominally in force to-day. The Quisling government of Vichy has never dared openly to attack or revoke it, though in fact it ignores many of its provisions.

IT IS FAIR TO SAY that in 1940 we and the French parted on pretty bitter terms. They felt that we had not sent them a large or powerful enough B.E.F., and that we had left them in the lurch at Dunkirk. Few of them believed we should carry on the war long after the evacuation. We, on our side, thought that the French had fought badly and had let us down by asking for a separate armistice which left *us* in the lurch. Since 1940 the French have learnt to value us rather more justly and generously. It is time for us, in our turn, to think rather less about the French collapse and rather more about subsequent resistance in France, and the fighting contributions made by Frenchmen at our side outside France, under General de Gaulle and, latterly, General Giraud as well.

In the interval between 1940 and now, unfortunately, some British forces and some French have fought against each other in several parts of the world outside France. It began with our sinking several French ships at Oran in Algeria, in July, 1940, for fear the Germans should get hold of the French fleet. Then at Dakar and, later, in Syria, in Madagascar, and during the first few days in North Africa we have been in battle against Frenchmen loyal to the Vichy Quisling government. On the other hand, throughout the Abyssinian, Libyan and Tunisian campaigns thousands of Frenchmen have fought by our side against the common enemy. Where they have opposed us, French troops and sailors have been obeying the order of superior officers weeded of pro-British elements by Vichy—which acted under *German* orders. Many of those who fought against us have since fought far more willingly by our side, with the knowledge that we are their friends.

ATTITUDE TO BOMBINGS.—If you are in doubt which of the two attitudes is more characteristics of the feelings of Frenchmen in France itself, recall a few facts. Remember how when the R.A.F. has bombed factories and airfields and railways used by the Germans in France, often killing and injuring French citizens in the process, the French still understand what we are doing so well that they help our airmen who bale out to escape, and pile with flowers the graves of British airmen who crash. Unfortunately, later bombing in thickly populated areas has caused increasingly heavy civilian casualties. It is only natural that these should have caused some resentment. Remember, too, the heroic French stand made at the Battle of Bir Hakeim and the way the French drove the Germans out of Corsica.

We need not doubt the goodwill of the vast majority of the people of France. Their feelings towards us are probably more cordial than at any time in the past, certainly more so than during the "phoney war" of 1939–40 or during the campaigns of 1914–18. The small, astoundingly brave minority who have led *active* resistance with in the Mother Country, have had behind them a growing proportion (lately up to 95 per cent) of the French people, who have *passively* resisted the Germans and their Vichy stooges. All the resisters, active and passive, have warm feelings towards this country, not only because we have the common aim of finishing off the Nazis, but because our broadcasts and leaflets have been an important means of keeping up their will to resist. Moreover, the example of British tenacity and British success has in itself been a spur to resistance. If Britain had failed, France might well have despaired.

THE 1940 DISASTER.—In 1940 our two countries suffered a joint military disaster. But while we continued the war undeterred, *unofficial* resistance in France and General de Gaulle's fighting forces, disowned by Vichy, were for a long time the only signs that France was un-subdued. At that time some of us, not without reason, blamed French politicians for failure to continue the war. Some of us also blamed certain French generals. A great many of us, however, blamed the French as a nation. **If you are one of these, remember that nothing is**

to be gained on either side by raking up the past, and secondly, that events since 1940 have proved what the spirit of France is like to-day.

The French remember an aspect of the war which we sometimes forget: the fact that Britain was not overrun in 1940 was due not only to Mr. Churchill and the "few" of the R.A.F., it was due also to our being protected by 20 miles of sea and by the Royal Navy. **If the Germans could have crossed our water-obstacle—the Channel—in the same way as they crossed the French water-obstacle—the river Meuse—are we quite sure that Britain would not have suffered the same immediate fate as France?** Thousands of our soldiers, sailors and airmen might have been carrying on the fight (as General de Gaulle had so long to carry it on) from outside the Mother Country, while inside the Mother Country the civil population might still be fighting back at German occupying troops (as the French have done) through sabotage, resistance and, when the time came, open revolt.

Thanks to the sea, this nightmare never occurred here, France *was* overrun with surprising speed, and the then French Cabinet decided by narrow majority *not* to carry on the war from North Africa. An armistice was signed and a puppet Government, which the French people have never recognized, was installed. The French are not proud of their misfortunes or of their Government's actions in 1940. But if you are rash enough to discuss them with a Frenchman, he will tell you that Britain is fortunate in being an island. France is not.

FRANCE SINCE 1940.—The greatest mistake you can make in going to France is to try to pick up the threads of the Anglo-French story where they were broken in June, 1940, as though France had stood still since that date. Try to realize something of what has happened since then. Apart from the general suffering and the general refusal to play with the Germans already referred to, two main facts should always be borne in mind in order to avoid misunderstanding.

First, that the Vichy Government, of which you have heard so much, has long been disowned as a German tool by almost every Frenchman. Secondly, that active resistance, starting immediately after the collapse from small isolated groups, has organized itself in the teeth of the Gestapo, the German army and Vichy, into a highly efficient network covering the whole of France. It recognized a central authority, and its members regarded themselves as soldiers under military orders. Frenchmen who have risked everything in these resistance groups feel that they have done all that lay in their power to redeem the disgrace of their country's collapse in 1940

34

by fighting on as our active allies. So, before reminding a Frenchman that France let us down in 1940, remind yourself that you may be speaking to one of the thousands of soldiers without uniform who have been fighting the same fight as you against the same enemy, but with fewer advantages.

ALLIED BLOCKADE.—The Germans and Vichy have tried hard to tell the French public that the shortages it has had to put up with were due to the Allied blockade. Their propaganda has, on the whole, misfired, and the average Frenchman attributes shortage to German looting. Here and there, however, some resentment may be felt about the results of the blockade. If you come across it, try to steer clear of discussions which, on details, can only be complicated and inconclusive. Total blockade was an absolute necessity in order to deny supplies of all kinds to the enemy, whose deliberate policy has been to reduce to a minimum the food available for local consumption in all occupied territories.

RELIEF.—You may, as already suggested, find some disappointment if relief supplies are slow in coming. **If you are questioned on this subject, explain that it is essential to defeat Germany as rapidly as possible, and consequently first priority on**

shipping of supplies must be given to military needs. At first this results in little shipping for relief supplies for liberated countries; but the civilians must have patience and believe that every effort is being made to bring them supplies as soon as possible.

FOOD.—The virtual starvation of France by the Germans will, as you have seen, make it impossible for us to "live on the country" in any sense during the first months. Later on conditions may change. If so, you will find in all parts of France what a difference good cooking can make to the simplest ingredients.

Don't give your food, clothing or other supplies to civilians or others. The Civil Affairs personnel will distribute supplies as soon as they become available. Giving your supplies away not only encourages further requests from civilians which cannot be satisfied, but puts an additional burden on the already over-burdened supply system.

DRINK.—In most parts of France you should boil all drinking water, whether from a tap, a well, a stream or a spring, unless your own M.O. tells you the contrary. Fresh milk you will not get at all; the French have not enough for their children. Tea, never widely drunk in France, is completely lacking, except for what the British and Americans my bring. Coffee is now almost wholly lacking.

Wines and spirits and, in parts of Northern France, the rough cider are the staple drinks. To-day they are rationed, and the Frenchman who gets his full ration is lucky. **If you should be offered wine or spirits, remember that this will be stronger drink than you are used to.** French beer is rather like our own light ale, but you will be fortunate if you come on any, and at present it is very much watered down.

WOMEN.——French women, both young and old, are far from shy and you will, if you are a man of sense, make them your friends. But do not mistake friendship for willingness to give you their favours. The same sort of girl with whom you can take liberties in England can be found in France, and the same sort of girl whom you would grossly offend in this country would be greatly offended if you were to "try anything on" in France.

The fathers, brothers and fiancés of French girls will often be unable to protect them because they are fighting the Germans or have been deported to Germany. Apart from any question of discipline, you are on your honour to behave to their womenfolk as you would wish them to behave to yours. If you do not, you will injure the reputation of the British soldier, by showing a worse example than the Germans, who at the start, at least, behaved with considerable restraint, though they later lapsed. As for the loose women, if you have noted the facts on page 12 about the prevalence of V.D., you will see good reasons for avoiding them.

ENTERTAINMENT.—French cinemas are not as modern as our own. In many of them smoking is not allowed for fear of fires. E.N.S.A. will, in due course, see after your entertainment; the films for ordinary French cinemas will have to be supplied by the Americans and ourselves for months to come. It would be almost as thoughtless to crowd the French out of their own cinemas or cafés as to buy all the food in the shops: you have had plenty of chances for recreation at home. For this reason some places of entertainment will be put out of bounds.

SPORTS.—The French are keen footballers, playing Soccer all over the country and Rugby largely in the towns, except those of the north and east. They have also produced some first-class tennis players. Hockey is played, especially in the North, and basket-ball is also popular. They do not play cricket or go in greatly for dog-racing, nor does horse-racing attract the same following that is does in this country. A sport on which the French people *are* particularly keen is cycle-racing: if your unit finds a chance to arrange a cycle-race fixture with the local champions, most of the neighbourhood will turn out to see the race. Another game familiar in almost every part of France is the French form of bowls, usually played on a small "dirt" ground instead of a bowling-green. French card-games are different from ours—and they are often played in an atmosphere of considerable excitement.

THE RULE OF THE ROAD.—You drive on the right of the road and NOT on the left. The main roads are straight and good, the side-roads are variable as our own. France to-day, thanks to the Germans, contains an undue proportion of the very old and the very young; the able-bodied have been largely deported. So do not drive through French towns and villages at a rate which means the inhabitants skipping out of your way. They may not be able to do so!

BEHAVIOUR.—The British Army represents in France to-day the British people. Any errors of conduct committed by individual soldiers will remain in French minds not simply as slur on a single man or a single unit but as "the way the British behave".

At the present time, owing to the effects of the German occupation, the French have suffered very much, and so are apt to be sensitive. It is up to us to show that little extra consideration which makes the difference between mere good will and real friendliness.

The French people, like our own, include both good and bad characters. You will be fortunate if you meet only the good Frenchmen; so do not grouse at the French in general if you should met a French "bad hat". There are probably one or two "bad hats" in every British unit.

The French will greet you on your arrival as a welcome and long-expected guest of their country. The good guest retains his welcome by making himself as little trouble as possible and doing all he can to help his hosts. If you can do this, you will be acting as a good Ally should; and in the process you may be increasing your own comfort.

FRENCH MONEY is reckoned on the decimal system, i.e. in tens. It is very simple to remember that 100 centimes go to a franc, and you will be told how many francs go to a £. The only complication you are likely to run across is that country people often count small sums, up to five francs, in "sous", that is five centimes; so "20 sous" will mean a franc, "100 sous" five francs.

All recent French coins have been made of aluminium or brass, but you are likely to get paper money for even the smallest sums. The Germans withdrew all the coins they could to make munitions.

There will be little at first for you to buy. When the time comes for buying things, try not to spend your money in a way which would encourage the old belief on the Continent that all Englishmen are both wealthy and foolish. **Don't be mean, but don't be extravagant either; if you are the prices are bound to go up, which would be bad luck on the local population and do you no good either.**

—DO'S—

The French are our friends. The Germans are our enemies and the enemies of France. Remember that the Germans individually often behaved well in France. We have got to behave better.

We are helping to free France. Thousands of Frenchmen have been shot in France for keeping alive the spirit of freedom. Let the French know that you realize the great part Frenchmen have played, both in the last war and in this war.

The French are more polite than most of us. Remember to call them "Monsieur, Madame, Mademoiselle", not just "Oy!"

Be patient if you find a Frenchman hard to understand— he is having difficulties too.

Remember to salute a French civilian or policeman when you address them. This is a normal form of politeness practised by the French. Salute when entering and leaving a private house, a café, or a shop.

Be natural, but don't make yourself too much at home till you are sure your French friends like it. Remember the intense suffering of the French since 1940. Make allowances for this.

—DONT'S—

Don't criticize the French Army's defeat of 1940. Many Frenchmen are convinced that they had a fine but insufficiently equipped army, not very well led. Many others themselves critical of the French Army of 1940, but they, too, will resent their own criticism coming from a foreigner.

Don't get into arguments about religion or politics. If a Frenchman raises one of the points which have strained Anglo-French relations since 1940, drop the matter. There are two sides to every question, but you don't want to take either.

Don't get drawn into discussions about the comparative merits and successes of the United Nations.

Don't, even if food is offered to you, eat the French out of house and home. If you do, someone may starve.

Don't mess things up even in an empty billet. Someone will live there after you.

Don't drink yourself silly. If you get the chance to drink wine, learn to "take it". The failure of some British troops to do so was the one point made against our men in France in 1939–40 and again in North Africa.

Don't sell or give away your food or equipment.

—MAKING YOURSELF UNDERSTOOD—

It is never very easy to make yourself understood at first in a foreign language, and it may be even less easy to understand a Frenchman's reply. If you find someone who knows a little English, speak very slowly and distinctly. If you are trying to understand French, get the speaker to say the words slowly, or (if that will help) to write them down clearly.

The words and phrases at the end of this booklet will NOT make you speak French "like a native", but they may help you out of difficulties until you learn more of the language. If a Frenchman cannot understand your pronunciation, point out the French word you want on the list.

You can't expect to learn all French grammar in one sentence, but you may notice that all French nouns are either masculine or feminine, and the adjective or article (i.e. "a" or "the") changes according to the gender of the noun which goes with it. Thus "my father" is "*mon* père"; "my mother" is "*ma* mère"; "A knife" is "*un* couteau"; "a fork" is "*une* fourchette". (English is the only language without these gender complications.)

—WORDS AND PHRASES—

Note: Under each French word is an English spelling in italics which reproduces as nearly as possible the sound of the French.

Good morning, or good afternoon, Good evening	Bonjour, Bonsoir *Bonjewer, Bonswa*
How do you do?	Comment allez-vous? *Commont-allay-voo?*
Goodbye	Au revoir *Oh-revwa*
I am, He is, She is	Je suis, Il est, Elle est *Sher swee, Eel ay, Ell ay*
We are, You are, They are	Nous sommes, Vous êtes, Ils (Elles) sont *Noo som, Vooze ate, Eel (El) sonn*
Is there anyone who speaks English?	Y a-t-il quelqu'un qui parle anglais? *Ee-ah-teel kel-kern key parl ongly?*
What is your name (address)	Quel est votre nom (votre adresse)? *Kel ay votrer nom (votrer adresse)?*
Please bring me, give me, lend me	Apportez-moi, donnez-moi, *apportay-mwah, donnay-mwah,* prêtez-moi, s'il vous plaît *praytay-mwah*
I like this very much	J'aime beaucoup ceci *Shame bocoo sirsee*
Hurry! Slowly!	Vite! Lentement! *Veet! Lontermon!*

Difficulties and Enquiries

What do you call this?	Comment s'appelle ceci?
	Comon sapel siresee?
I don't understand	Je ne comprends pas
	Sher ner compron pah
Do you understand?	Comprenez-vous?
	Comprenay voo?
Please speak slowly (write it down)	Parlez lentement,
	Parlay lontermon,
	(écrivez-le),
	ekreevay-ler,
	s'il vous plait
	seal voo play
What nationality are you?	De quelle nationalité êtes-vous?
	Der kell nass-ee-onalitay ate voo?
Are you French? German?	Etes-vous Français? Allemand?
	Ate voo Fronsay? Allmon?
Have you seen any soldiers (the enemy)?	Avez-vous vu des soldats (l'ennemi)?
	Avay voo view day soldah (lenmee)?
What kind of soldiers?	Quelle sorte de soldats?
	Kell sort der soldah?
Are the trees in that wood thick?	Ce bois est-il épais?
	Sir bwah ate-eel epay?
Can we sleep in your barn (outbuildings)?	Pouvons-nous dormir dans votre grange
	Poovon noo dormeer dong votrer gronge
	(vos hangars)?
	(voze hongar)?
Where is the Town Hall (Police Station)?	Ou est la mairie
	Oo ay lah mary
	(le Commissariat de Police)?
	(ler Commissariah der poleece)?

Travelling by Road

Is this the way to _____?

Est-ce le chemin pour _____?
Ay sir ler shman poor _____?

Which is this the way to _____?

Quel est le chemin pour _____?
Kell ay ler shman poor _____?

How far is it to _____?

A quelle distance est _____?
Ar kell deeestons ay _____?

Will you guide me, please?

Voulez-vous me conduire, si'il vous plaît?
Voolay-voo mer condweer seal vous play?

Where does this road lead to?

Voulez-vous me conduire, si'il vous plaît?
Voolay-voo mer condweer seal vous play?

Where am I now? Show me on this map

Où mène cette route?
Oo mane set root

Is this road clear?

Cette route est-elle ouverte?
Set root ate ell oovairt?

I am lost

Je suis perdu
Sher swee pairdoo

I want to go (return) to _____

Je voudrais aller (rentrer) à _____
Sher voodray allay (rontray) ar

Stop! Go back (reverse)!

Arrêtez! En arrière!
Arrettay! On arree-air!

Gon on!

En avant!
On avon!

Danger!

Danger!
Donjay!

Bicycle, horse, mule, cart

La bicyclette (le vélo), Le cheval,
Lar bee-see-clet (ler vailo), Ler sheval,
Le mulet, la charrette
Le mewlay, lar sharret

Car Repairs

My car (lorry, truck) has broken down	Ma voiture (mon camion) est en panne *Mar vwattewer (mom cam-ee-on) at on pàn*
Where is the nearest garage?	Où est le garage le plus proche? *Oo ay ler garage ler ploo prosh*
I need petrol (oil, water)	J'ai besoin d'essence (d'huile, d'eau) *Shay bes-wann dessonce (dweel, doe)*
Can you lend me some tools?	Pouvez-vous me prêter des outils? *Poovay-voo mer praytay daze oottee?*

Accommodation; Baths

Where can I get a bed for tonight?	Où pourrai-je coucher cette nuit? *Oo poor-age cooshay set nwee*
These are my (our) billets	Je suis logé (nous sommes logés) ici *Sher swee lowjay (noo som lowjay) eesee*
May I (we) come in?	Peut-on entrer? *Purt-on entray?*
I shall be returning late (leaving early)	Je rentrerai tard, (partirai de bonne heure) *Sher rontrerat tar, (parteray der bon urr*
Can we have something to eat (drink)?	Pouvons-nous manger (boire)? *Poovon-noo monjay (bwarr)*
May I have a key?	Puis-je avoir la clef)? *Pweege avwarr lar clay?*
A hot bath, Soap, Towel	Un bain chaud, Le savon, La serviettè *Urn ban show, ler savon, lar serviettè*
Lavatory, Cloakroom, Dining-rooom	La toilette, Le vestiaire, La salle à manger *Lar twahlet, Ler vestayre, Lar sal ar monjay*

Food, Drink

Where can I eat (drink)?	Où peut-on manger (boire)? *Oo purt-on monjay (bwarr)?*
May I have breakfast (dinner, supper)?	Puis-je avoir le petit déjeuner *Pweege avwarr let p'tee* (déjeuner, diner)? *(day-shuon-ay, deenay)*
How much a kilo (litre)?	Combien le kilo (le litre)? *Combyang ler keelo (ler leetr)?*
Wine, Cider, Beer	Le vin, Le cidre, La bière *Ler vang, Ler ceedrer, Lar beeyare*
The bill please	L'addition, s'il vous plaît *Lad-issy-on, seal voo play*

Accidents

Fetch a doctor, please	Allez chercher un médecin, s'il vous plaît *Allay shairshay urn maidsang seal voo plait*
Come and help quickly	Venez vite aider *Venay veet aiday*
There has been an accident	Il y a eu un accident *Eel-ee-ah-ewe urn ack-see-dong*
I have been wounded (injured)	Je suis blessé *Sher swee blessay*
Artery, Tourniquet	L'artère, le tourniquet *Lartare, ler toor-ne-kay*
Bring cold (boiling) water	Apportez de l'eau froide (bouillante) *Apportay der lo frwahd (boo-ee-ont)*

50

—WEIGHTS AND MEASURES—

These are based on the decimal Metric System used in most European countries. This is simpler than our British system, since units are all multiples of ten. The equivalents given are *approximate only*—for quick reckoning.

Length

1 Centimetre (cm.)	1 Centimètre	= two-fifths of an inch
1 Metre (m = 100 cms.)	1 Mètre	= 3ft. 3ins.
1 Kilometre (km = 1,000 m.)	1 Kilomètre	= five-eights of a mile

To convert *centimetres into inches*—multiply by 4 and divide the result by 10
(1 inch = 2½ cms. 1 foot = 30 cms.)
To convert *metres into yards*—add one-ninth the number of metres
(1 yard = nine-tenths of a metre)
To convert *kilometres into miles*—divide the kms. by 8 and multiply the result by 5
(1 mile = just over 1½ kms.)

Weight

1 Gram (g.)	1 Gramme	= 15½ grains
1 Kilogram (kg. = 1,000 gs.)	1 Kilogramme (or Kilo.)	= 2 lb. 3 oz.
1 Ton	1 Tonne	= 1,016 kilos.

To convert *kilograms into pounds*—double and then add one-tenth of the result
(1 lb. = roughly half a kilo, 1 cwt. = 50 kilos.)

Area

1 Hectare   1 Hectare   = nearly 2½ acres

To convert *hectares into acres*—multiply by 5 divide by 2
(1 acre = two-fifths hectare.)

Liquid Capacity

1 Litre   1 Litre   = 1¾ pints

To convert *litres into pints*—add half, and then a half of the half
(¾ pints = just over half a litre.)
To convert *litres into gallons*—divide by 5
(1 gallon = 4½ litres.)

Heat

The measurement used is called Centigrade, by which water freezes at 0 degrees
(instead of our 32° Fahrenheit) and boils at 100° (instead of our 212° Fahrenheit).
Normal body temperature is 37°.
To convert *Centigrade into Fahrenheit*—double, subtract onetenth of the result and
add 32. (100° F. = about 38°.)

—SECURITY NOTE—

Now is the time for you to realize that all that you have learnt about security during your training at home applies with equal force to operations overseas. In fact, those of you who have already seen foreign service will be able to tell the others that security is, for the reasons that follow, even more important overseas than in the U.K.

One of the most important reasons for this is that you have moved and will continue to move into areas which have been occupied by the enemy for a long time. **The enemy will spare no pains to leave behind, scattered among the civilian population, agents, saboteurs and propagandists who will be a continual threat to our security.**

Their numbers will greatly exceed anything with which we have had to cope in the past—and it will be infinitely more difficult to detect them. Added to this, the enemy will have prepared channels of communications for the use of his agents, and which he may well be able to use long after actual hostilities have ceased.

So there must be no relaxation of security-mindedness and suspicious alertness, even in those areas where the battle has moved on and comparatively peaceful conditions may prevail. In these areas particularly you must be on your guard.

As you have been told so often, personal responsibility is the key-note of good security. On the individual discretion of each British and Allied soldier depends the security of the whole Army. This applies particularly to your relations with the civil population. **Do not forget that far more Europeans understand English than is popularly supposed. So be very careful what you say—not only to civilians, but to each other in their hearing.**

Speech on the telephone may have special dangers. Security of documents will be of more than usual importance. Even the letters you receive from home, or the addresses on letters you receive from your friends in the same expeditionary force, may contain information which the Enemy will want to know.

You should keep a particular look-out for suspects, and report immediately any cases which you may come across to your Unit Security Officer or to a Field Security N.C.O. Pay particular attention to the checking of identity documents, and do not hesitate to detain, if necessary by force, any suspicious individuals. Some of these may be disguised as British officers or men; and it is no unlikely that the beautiful spy will come into her own again.

The danger of sabotage will also be considerable. This means that when you are guarding material or equipment, your job will be particularly important; and that you must continue to take great care of your personal weapons and equipment.

You must expect that propaganda will be directed to driving a wedge between the Allies, for instance, by attempting to promote anti-Russian feeling. There may also be attempts to organize sympathy for the German people. This propaganda, which may be in many forms—some crude and obvious, but some subtle and hard to recognize—will be directed by enemy sympathisers and agents against your morale. Women are clever at this sort of work, and will no doubt often be used. Do not allow yourself to be affected by any of this. You have a job to do—and you must see it through with good will and determination.

Life in ex-German Europe will demand your vigilance, alertness and self-confidence. These must be used in applying with common sense the security principles you have been taught.

—ROAD SIGNS—

1. Gutter

2. Sharp Turn

3. Cross-Roads

4. Unguarded Level Crossing

5. One-Way Road or Entry Prohibited

6. Dangers other than those indicated by signs 1 to 4

7. Motor Vehicles Prohibited

8. Weight Limit

9. Maximum Speed

10. Overtaking Prohibited

11. Parking Prohibited

12. Stopping Prohibited